When Someone You Love Dies

When Someone You Love Dies

This book belongs to _____

By Cynthia A. Snyder, PhD
Illustrations by Dawn Pardun
©2011

WestBow
PRESS
A DIVISION OF THOMAS NELSON

WestBow Press books may be ordered through booksellers or by contacting:

WestBow Press
A Division of Thomas Nelson
1663 Liberty Drive
Bloomington, IN 47403
www.westbowpress.com
1-(866) 928-1240

Because of the dynamic nature of the Internet, any web addresses or links contained in this book may have changed since publication and may no longer be valid. The views expressed in this work are solely those of the author and do not necessarily reflect the views of the publisher, and the publisher hereby disclaims any responsibility for them.

Certain stock imagery © Thinkstock.
Any people depicted in stock imagery provided by Thinkstock are models, and such images are being used for illustrative purposes only.

ISBN: 978-1-4497-3118-2 (e)
ISBN: 978-1-4497-3117-5 (sc)

Library of Congress Control Number: 2011960335

Printed in the United States of America

WestBow Press rev. date: 12/6/2011

A Word to Parents

Our society is uneasy with the reality of personal death. We idolize youth and beauty, hiding death behind euphemisms and rituals that most children of pre-school and elementary age do not understand.

The intent of this book is to explain the death of a loved one to children in plain language that they can understand. Children are much more frightened of the mysterious and the unexplained than they are if they understand the natural process of death and the rituals we use to say "good-bye" to a loved one who has died.

Your job as a parent or a "best grown-up friend" is crucial: to make sure that you do not leave your child alone with death. Simply by reading this book with your child, you can help dispel the fears that a child inevitably encounters when faced with the death of someone they love. This book will not answer every child's every question, but it will give you a starting point to help your child begin to grasp the reality of death and yet still be able to nurture hope in his heart.

By explaining what ancient peoples called "the Great Circle of Life" --- we come from God, we live, and then we return to God --- we can release our children from the fears of the mysterious and the unknown and give them the precious gift of hope.

Part I:

What Happens When Someone Dies

When a loved one dies, most children have many questions. This book can help you to understand more about what is happening during this sad time. It can also help to ask your mom or dad or your best grown-up friend to read the book with you. They can talk about your questions, your feelings, and the things that are happening. This can make some of the confused and lonely feelings go away and can make you feel less afraid.

Have you ever seen a butterfly, flying beautiful and free?

A butterfly begins its life as a caterpillar. That's right!
A small, fuzzy, green caterpillar finds a leaf or a twig and
latches on to it. The caterpillar spins a cocoon around its
whole body, and then it waits. After a few days, the cocoon
dies and splits open. The butterfly comes out of the cocoon
and stretches its beautiful wings and flies away.

Sometimes a person who you love very much dies.
Perhaps he had been sick for a long time, or maybe she
died suddenly, like in a car accident.

Whichever way the person died, it is a very sad time.

Sad times, like happy times, are normal parts of our lives.
Sad times happen to everyone, not just to you.

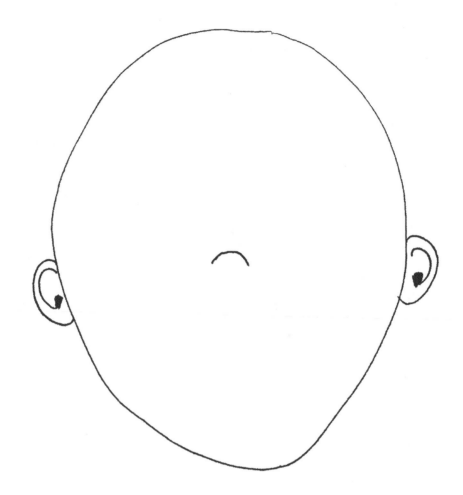

During this sad time, there are many things going on and the grown-ups you love can be very busy. They are busy making plans to say good-bye to the person who has died.

In fact, they may seem to be so busy that you might feel a little bit ignored and like no one has any time for you even if you feel confused and afraid. This might make you feel lonely. It might make you feel afraid or even mad at God. That's OK. God knows and loves your heart, and He understands your feelings. No matter what you feel, God will <u>not</u> get mad at you. Can you draw a picture of your face that shows how you feel right now?

12

No grown-up ignores you on purpose. Many adults know that you are feeling confused, lonely, and a little bit afraid. It's usually just that they don't know what to say to you to make you feel better. Even grown-ups can feel lonely and scared when someone they love dies.

Sometimes it's up to you to ask your important questions of a grown-up who you love and trust. Or you can just ask them to read this book with you.

When children find out that someone they love has died, often one of their first questions is "What does it mean to die?"

Sometimes, you can feel confused just by the words that some people use. Instead of saying that someone has died, they might say he has "passed on" or "passed away". You might think, "Well, where did he pass on to? Did she go somewhere else? "

When grown-ups say that a person has "passed away", they simply mean that he has died.

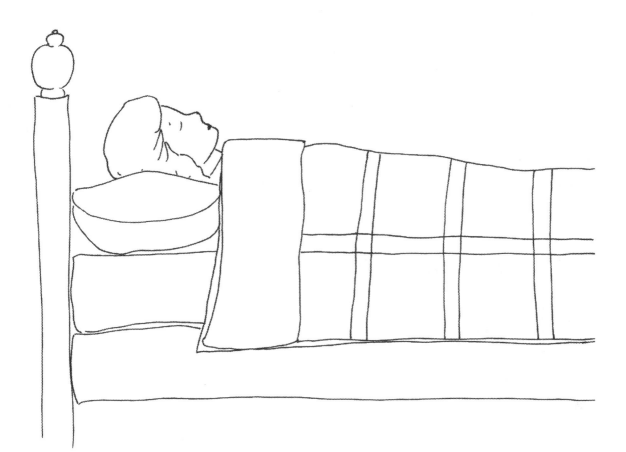

When someone you love dies, his body doesn't work anymore. He doesn't get thirsty or hungry, he doesn't breathe anymore, and he doesn't move. He doesn't feel any pain, and he doesn't feel afraid.

A dead person's body looks a lot like she is asleep. She is very peaceful and still.

Remember the caterpillar and his cocoon?

It is much the same when a person dies. His body – like the caterpillar's cocoon – simply doesn't work anymore. But the <u>spirit</u> of the person you love is still very much alive. Like the living butterfly that came out of its dead cocoon, the spirit of the person who died leaves its old body behind and flies home to God – beautiful and free.

16

But what is a spirit, anyway?

A spirit is not a ghost or a monster or anything scary.
Every person on earth has a spirit – even you and me.

17

Your spirit is that invisible part inside of you that makes you who you are.

Do you like to tell knock-knock jokes and make people laugh? Do you like to help your mom or dad bake cookies or wash the car? Do you like to play with your brothers or sisters? Do you like to sing? Do you like to cuddle close to your grandpa or grandma and watch TV together? Do you love to snuggle with your pet?

All of these things put together help make who you are on the inside. All of these things are part of your spirit.

Draw some pictures of other things that are part of who you are, other things that are part of your spirit. Maybe you like to play ball with your dog, or perhaps you like to listen to the stories that your mom or dad tell you. Do you like to play with floating toys while you are taking a bath?

I'll bet that you can think of lots of things that make up that invisible part of you: your spirit.

20

Part II:

What Happens When Someone Dies

Some people die in a hospital, some die in a nursing home, and some die in their own homes. No matter where they die, they will all go to a <u>funeral home</u> where they will be taken care of by a <u>funeral director</u>.

A funeral home is a safe place for the body of the person you love to be. It is a place where your loved one's body will wait until it is time for the <u>funeral</u>.

The <u>funeral director</u> is a man or a woman who is in charge of the funeral home. He talks to the family and helps them decide what kind of <u>funeral</u> they want and where it will be.

There are two kinds of funerals that the family of your loved one might choose. One kind of funeral is a <u>burial</u> and the second kind is <u>cremation</u>.

The funeral director makes sure that the body of someone who has died is treated with respect and care. But his most important job is to help the family and friends say "good-bye" to the person who died.

For a burial, the funeral director makes sure that your loved one's body is washed and dressed up in their best clothes and that their hair is also washed and fixed so that it looks nice. The last thing that the funeral director does is to lay your loved one's body in a casket, sometimes called a coffin.

A casket or coffin is both a long box with a lid on it and a comfortable bed at the same time. The body of your loved one is laid down in the casket with his head resting on a soft pillow. Sometimes the lid of the casket is left open during the funeral so that you can see the person's face. Other times, the lid is kept closed.

Draw your own picture here.

25

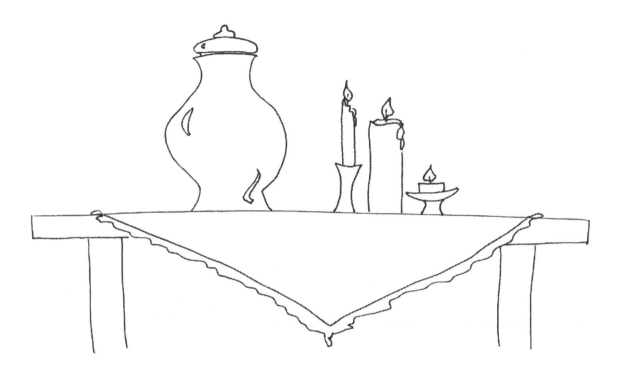

The second way that the funeral director might make your loved one ready for his funeral is called <u>cremation</u>.

When a body is cremated, it is carefully burned. When a piece of wood is burned, it turns into ashes. The same thing happens when a human body is burned: it, too, turns into ashes.

Remember, when your loved one died, his body stopped working. His spirit is no longer living in his body, so he feels no pain and he is not afraid.

When your loved one's body has been cremated, the ashes are carefully placed into a special container. The container might be a special box or a vase that is called an urn. The container is sealed tight to keep the ashes safely inside.

If the family has decided to cremate your loved one's body, they then choose what to do with his ashes. They might bury the ashes in a grave, or they might keep the container in a safe and special place, or they might decide to scatter the ashes in a place that was special to the person who died. If they decide to scatter the ashes, the ashes will fly away free upon God's wind – as free as the butterfly.

After the funeral director and his helpers are finished getting your loved one's body ready, it is time for the <u>funeral</u>.

A <u>funeral</u> is kind of like a quiet party. The guests are the family and friends who loved the person who died. The funeral is the time when family and friends come together to celebrate the life of the person who died. They come to pray and to say "I love you" and "I will miss you" and "good-bye". They also come to the funeral so you won't feel so alone.

When you come to the funeral, the body of the person who died will be in the casket or her ashes will be in the special container. Even though it is sad to see someone we care about in a casket or an urn, we can still have happy memories about the special times you shared with the person who died.

Many people send beautiful flowers to the funeral to show sympathy. When they show sympathy, they are saying, "I am very sorry that someone you love has died, and I will miss them, too."

At the funeral, it helps to be near people who care not only about the person who died, but who also care about you.

The funeral is usually led by a pastor, a priest, or a rabbi. Who leads the funeral depends on what kind of church your loved one or his family went to. There might be music and special prayers. Sometimes, other people will get up to talk about their good memories of the person who has died. The funeral is a time for "sharing of memories".

You, too, can get up and share a special memory of a good time that you shared with the person who died.

After the first part of the funeral is over, some people will carry the casket to a special car called a <u>hearse</u>. The funeral director and his helpers drive the hearse to the <u>cemetery</u>. The other people who came to the funeral get into their own cars and follow the hearse. They all turn their car lights on, and sometimes police officers ride alongside on their motorcycles. This is called a <u>funeral</u> <u>procession</u>. A funeral procession is like a slow, quiet parade to show others how much we love the person who died.

While we are driving in the funeral procession, other people may be out driving their cars too, doing ordinary things like going to school or going to the grocery store. These people did not know your loved one who died and were not at the funeral, but they can see that a line of cars with their lights turned on is a funeral procession. Usually these drivers will pull their cars over to the side of the road and stop to wait for the funeral procession to go by.

By doing this, these strangers are sending you a silent message: "We can see that someone you loved has died. We are sorry for your loss of this important person in your life."

The funeral director drives the hearse – and the funeral procession follows – to a <u>cemetery</u>.

A cemetery is like a pretty park, with trees, grass, flowers, birds and squirrels. But it is not a park that has swings and monkey-bars and other playthings. A cemetery is a special place set aside where people are buried when they die.

After everyone has arrived at the cemetery, the casket
is placed next to the grave. Sometimes, the family will
decide to bury the container holding their loved one's
ashes. Other times, the container is not buried.
A grave is a special hole where the casket or the container
of ashes will be buried.

Now is the time for the second part of the funeral. It is called the <u>graveside</u> <u>service</u>. The pastor or priest or rabbi will say some more things and pray some more prayers. Someone might read a poem or some words from the Bible. There might be some more music.

If your loved one was in our country's military service during his life, soldiers sometimes come to the graveside service. Just before the service is over, the soldiers will fire their rifles into the air. Don't be afraid if this happens. The soldiers are firing their rifles into the sky, not at anyone. Then they take the American flag that has been put on the casket, fold it up very carefully, and give it to a family member. This is a very special ceremony to thank your loved one for helping our country.

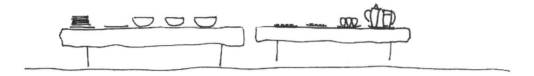

This is the end of the funeral, and everyone will leave either to go home or to gather together again to share a meal.

After the people leave the graveside service, some people who work for the cemetery will lower the casket into the grave and fill it in with dirt. Soon, soft grass will grow over the grave.

After this, the family will place a special marker on the grave that will last for a long, long time. It is called a headstone. The headstone will have words on it to tell people who is buried there, when she was born, and when she died. So, you will always be able to know exactly where your loved one's grave is, and you will be able to go back to see it any time you want. Many people bring flowers to lay on the grave when they visit. The flowers are a silent message, too: "We miss you, and we have not forgotten you."

Now is a good time to think about your special memories of your loved one who died. It might be a quiet memory of when he did something especially kind or helpful when someone else was having trouble. You might remember how he could make you laugh just because he could say something funny. Or how she enjoyed watching her favorite TV shows or how he liked to sing. You might remember how much he liked to go fishing, or how he would have you stand on his feet and then pretend that you were dancing together.

Can you draw a picture of one of your special memories?

Best of all, you can remember how much that special person who died loved you and your family and friends. That's the most special memory of all.

No one knows exactly what heaven looks like, but the Bible tells us that it is a wonderful place. God has promised us that when we come to live in heaven, we will never again be sad or hurting. He promised us that He will wipe every tear away from our eyes. Instead, we will always be happy and never again be frightened or sad. Won't that be great?

God has said that when someone comes to live with Him in heaven, everyone there will celebrate! Just imagine God and Jesus saying, "We're so glad you are here! Welcome!"

Close your eyes and imagine your loved one in heaven. What do you think she is doing? Is she singing beautiful songs with friends? Is he going fishing with Jesus? Can you draw a picture of what you imagine your loved one is doing in heaven?

The next few pages are for you.

When someone they love dies, many children do not get a chance to say "good-bye" and "I'll miss you" and "I love you". If you want to, you can use the next page to write a little letter or draw some special picture for the person who died. When you are done, give it to a grown-up. He or she will then give it to the pastor, and the pastor will put your letter or picture into the casket with your loved one for you.

And remember: although this is a sad time, you can also have happiness. Remember the butterfly. Your loved one's spirit has flown home to God – and that's the very best place to be.